A Slither

To Susan,
Love

~~Alison Lock~~

Alison

Indigo Dreams Publishing

First Edition: A Slither Of Air
First published in Great Britain in 2011 by:
Indigo Dreams Publishing
132 Hinckley Road
Stoney Stanton
Leicestershire
LE9 4LN

www.indigodreams.co.uk

Alison Lock has asserted her right under the Copyright, Designs and Patents Act 1988 to be identified as the author of this work.

ISBN 978-1-907401-43-5

British Library Cataloguing in Publication Data. A CIP record for this book can be obtained from the British Library.

Designed and typeset in Palatino Linotype by Indigo Dreams.

Cover design by Ronnie Goodyer at Indigo Dreams.

Printed and bound in Great Britain by Imprint Academic, Exeter.

'... holding its pattern for one little space
of time against the wood like fragile lace.'

from *'First Snow'* – Jane Tyson Clement

Acknowledgements

I would like to thank those who have supported me in bringing this collection together, especially Ken whose encouraging words gave me the confidence I needed, to Kay for listening, to Sue for the author photograph and my many other friends who came on the journey with me.

To my family and especially to Ian whose support has been immeasurable.

Thanks also to Ronnie and Dawn at Indigo Dreams for believing in me and for their evident enthusiasm for poetry. This collection comes as a result of winning the Indigo Dreams 2010 Collection prize.

Versions of many of the poems in this collection have appeared in anthologies, in poetry magazines or as winners in poetry competitions. These include The Word at York St. John University, Quaker Voices, Crab Lines Summer Anthology, Visible Breath, Reach Poetry, Dreamcatcher and Soul Feathers – Macmillan Cancer Care Anthology.

CONTENTS

A Slither Of Air

A Slither Of Air

We speak
through a slither of air
gulls hover
bringing your ocean to me
filling the deep well of my living
room. I see the beach where
your breath is fearless and

over my shoulder
a memory of you running blind
brakes screeching
like the sea birds now.

My heart beat then
and later to a rhythm that defined you.

Now your feet sink into the sand as
you press the text
of your life
into my uncoiled
ear.

Ladybird, Ladybird

I stop the sh sh across my page

to watch a squirrel nuzzle the ground
all auburn fuzz, nose down
re- checking the co-ordinates
on a mental map for a nut called X

the shrubs wear their prettiest bonnets
of permed seed heads, legs
black stockinged from stalking
the late summer rains

the lawn has had its last trim of the year
concentric, whorled
shaved into an Italianate maze.

A four spotted ladybird comes to my sill
I lend her my pen for a bridge
I am curious
now there are six spots
two on the edge of her shell
as if about to fall off, and they do
with a shiver, she splits

into a pair of dash away wings
taking her back to her home.

I carry on with the sh sh across my page.

Last Night I Woke Inside A Dream

Last night I woke inside a dream
I was staying at your house
where you made me tea
of steamed plaice
with all the bones taken out
you gave me milk and honey
in a proper cup and saucer
we podded peas together
and while they boiled
you told me a story
my head on your shoulder
your arm around me
the scent of sugared almonds
on your skin.
Then you pressed your lips to my cheek
pulled a satin quilt around me
I fell back to sleep on a bed
of the softest feathers.

The Mistletoe Collector

We found it in the loft
after you had died.
The label on the back
said 'Mistletoe collector' 1845.

The picture strained
inside a worm holed frame
was of a stump of a tree
from which hung a greedy vine.

Below it was a girl
whose arms were weighted down
with berried leaves that draped
the length of her gown

now off-white, beribboned,
she waited for a kiss
but no-one saw her in the attic
so she never had her wish.

Summer Solstice

It started with a single bird in a navy blue sky when it seemed
that the ghost-suns of twilight had only just disappeared.
Perhaps that's how it always is, the slide

from sleep to wake in a suspect range of colours.
After all, the day begins with the only certainty
of a number on a calendar, but you can be sure

that the Earth knows. Inclining towards the sun, rumbling
in her misty heaven, she shakes, sighs, blinks, as if caught
unawares. Checks her surface for a tracery of fate,

a man-made destiny, a holy kismet, each maw,
cleft, fissure, rib of mountain, rift of valley,
every notch in the vertebrae of the archipelagos,

the stately skulls of continents, the musculature
of grinding Tectonic brutes. Then they meet
full-on. The Roman sun-standing who winks

at first light, inflecting pulses of synchronicity
profusing colours that seep and merge until the earth
is flooded with tints of midsummer calendula.

A chorus erupts in a mighty genesis. They gather,
emergent creatures together, catching their first breath
with a grand pranayama they rise in salutation to the sun.

Under The Duvet

Water drops
　　　falling on roof tops
a steady rhythmic plash
　　　with a hint
of glockenspiel precision.

　　　Semibreves echo
oval notes
　　　aloof, random, remote
until an east wind
　　　booms

a rumpus starts
　　　in the pit
while a bar of crotchets
　　　trills a nervous flute
spit- flutter

　　　the window pane.
Outside, in the trees
　　　strings vibrate
leaves pluck
　　　one by one by whistle one.

Shadows curse
　　　fade and fall
an aural blanket
　　　envelops the dark
but the Insider

is listening
from under
her duvet
enjoying the orchestra
spinning its plates.

Patchwork

I remember
those first baby stitches
cast on tight
to catch the unravelling
gone too far
as we danced
through a night of fire.

Later I found
sand blown particles
had seeded the rib
of my harlequin stole
and the patches
mis-matched
tell our tale
like the iridescent twine
that traced our path
through a closed-up market
on our way
to a lunchtime of jazz.

I remember
those twill strands
that came from a hank
in the last and final sale
round the corner
from the place
where we first met.

I knew they'd come in
some day
even those tight spheres
of unpicked ringlet yarn
from the depths
of the darners chest
reborn
to make this cloak
of plied diamonds
that folds around
you and me
and nestles our tiny prince
to my breast.

As we walk the tide line
his bobble head nods
within a shawl
of flapping wings
as together
we three
catch the rhythm of the sea
wrapping
its visceral length around us.

Sea Swan

Her loved ones
sleep the naked moon
white crescents
etched on black.

As she drifts and dips
her beak turns
a swarm of creatures
skitter the sand.

Her wingspan scoops
a green under-layer
drips, rippling
her regal silhouette.

Unruffled
her deep black rudders
shift, as seamless
as her gimlet eye

spots a flip
then with precision
her neck re-forms
in a graceful arch.

Walking A White Page

I follow impressions, indents
crushes of temporary evidence

tiny shallow graves
hollowed by the winter light

their purity cut and preserved
until the next puddling

of the wish wash rain.
A flash of sun opens, shuts, blinds

batting up and down in monochrome.
I brush away the whiskery flakes

my skin brittles, capillaries burst
crack like a pack of dried mud

now the snow is spotted red
my pace quickens

the knowing look of ewes
hunkered under their oilskins

chewing cross-wise, their doe eyes
say they have seen nothing

but the ground around is flecked
with more blood than from a dog's cut paw

 By luck, I find a rabbit's foot
           – severed, and a fine plucked skut

entrails, strewn carelessly
spilled onto the fresh white page.

North By North Sea

I have seen them.
Dinosaurs
virtually every vertebra intact
chasing a line in the sand
their permanence preserved in rock
not dead
but fossilised
likely to wake
on a well-aged moon
when the sea
that sleek black splash
high-fives on the tide
creeps up the beach,
all stealth
in its robe of navy and white
trimming a foamy bravado
enough spittle
to rehydrate a national ossuary.

Once plumped
those prehistoric tails
play flick-tag
playful as lambs
watched over
by the high ridged rocks
their pride in a pattern
of dignified frowns
of A-symmetrical synclines
anticlines all in a row.

Above are a brooding
trick of slit-eyes
arrow heads pointing
ready to shoot back in time
by a millennia or two
way before the rolling
of Anglo-Saxon heads
or the Celts turned their backs
on the Normans
drawing grey crayon lines
of battlements
along the Northumbrian coast.

Higher still
above the cliffs, the rocks, the beach
high in the clear North Sea sky
I see a kite
a dragon kite
flown by a child
whose upper hand guides the string
in a stunt of swirls
writing his name in the sky.

Piano Lesson

Under my palms are apples, skin red,
I feel their waxy blush as I hold them
in a tight but nervous caress.

I must not let them fall onto the keys
as my hands arch in a grip, they tip
over scales, throw arpeggios this way and that.

'Have you practiced at all this week?' she asks
with a ruler quiver-held on a crotchet
her swollen feet rest on the bar of my stool

enclosed in their thick sausage stockings.
My fingers pause then 'Thwack'- they sting
all the way down to my green bones.

Rag And Bone

'Any old rags,' she calls,
pulling a cart, ringing her bell.
It is always morning back then
where the white sun
makes the tarmac black.

She takes my bag of rags.
I grab the stream-filled pouch.

'Poor little fish,' Mother says
when she sees
the ragged fin
the nick in the tail.

So I let go
releasing long slivers of silver.

As the goldfish is freed
it gives me a dorsal wave.

Map Makers

Above are the boulderers
spider men and women
whose keen eyes
look to angle and bag.
Like web makers they cast tripwires
they tap, pin, pull claws
to pocket another munro.

Below them the mountain ash
nods at their jubilance.
An otter in the stream sees the blue
flick flick of the kingfisher's morse
the wavering sparrows rock
in the rowan-hipped trees
a wren stabs a maggot for its tea.

High in the sky
a peregrine eyes a jay- blue skull
as it abseils down on a silken thread
like the grouse who flaps euphoric
free of its heather fleece
sputtering up and up
into the quartz-grey uncharted sky.

Insomnia

As I look through a telescope
the wrong way
my face sucked into the fat funnel end
I become a distant circle in the thrall
of blinking satellites.
Shaken glitter on fingered glue

at first static, fixed by a central star
then slid by the laws of time
this way and that
never to a regular rhythm
random like the flecking moths
in a faint constellation of night.

I burrow further into seams of warrens
threaded lines of punctured holes
the bric-a-brac of night.
I cling to remnants
that in the rips of time disintegrate
littering the air with spangled thoughts

their fine wefts I brush from my face.
In time the spyglass magnifies
for dawn to hark the starlings chitter
while hum-drone traffic ploughs the air.
Only then does the wood pigeon settle
deep inside her vibrant throat.

At The Mela

Bhaji, bhangra, bollywood, hip hop
segments of whole sugar cane.
I am pulled from stall to stall
by buds of colour and taste.

I look down at my cherub
my hand on the string
of his red balloon. But here
is a flat jellyfish the size of his fist.
The moment folds, crushing
seconds into micro seconds,
long enough to be seared,
cleaved from heart to bowel.

His curls flash and surf the crowd.
I hear the sound of a thrush
in the bush whose warbled tune
puts suspicion in my mind.
I scream but the rhythm
of the base beat mutes me.
I flick an index of faces
Have you, have you, have you seen?

Then he appears just there
with his toffee-like grin
that I want to smash
and squash and shake
I love him so much.

Kandahar

A boy finds a fallen star

from a pocket of treasures
his hand reaches out

pulls the loop that is trip-wired
to a hurricane, it lifts him high

higher to a crescent of incandescence
then down he flitters in a shower

of pomegranate seeds seeping the ground
sweet red, dark red, black red.

Now there is light, swinging bright
he waves back with a bound stub

as if reaching for a moonbeam.

The Shoe Rack

On the rack today are the shoes
of an actor who played the Khalif

pantomime originals slipper soled
for gliding the magic carpet

filled with applause their arches
accentuate moments of triumph.

Barely discernible are the thumbprints
of the servant who tidies them away.

Just inside the door are the shoes of a poet
inner soles well worn

they are wide and beige
loafish in a ciabatta sort of way

shoes that impress fine words
into the lug-holes of the Earth.

The brogues of Grandfather Barry
are highly buffed just as they were

when he arrived from over the sea
in 1923. Spit and polish.

Nicely Sunday. They smell of leather
and parsnips cooked to a tee.

Then there are the satin dainties.
Visiting maiden's called Laura, Natalie, Becky

who come to woo my sons
with their dulcimers and fine-tuned harps.

Tied with frayed ribbons
they shift in the slightest breeze.

And high on the wall is a shoe
that once shod a Carpathian horse.

Unbridled now, barefoot
she gallops the soft forest floor

and I am left with a metal curve
filled to the brim with luck.

In The Gandhi Room

A bird falls from the eaves
of my night window
young, eager to catch the wind
flapping, skitting up
lifting above a barrage of wake time.
It misses but lands plum
into my dream catcher's net.

Shaft feathers, baby soft plumage
spike beak, scrag ribs
fight against the woven sheath
that winds tighter and tighter around its beat.

And Gandhi says
there is no life without courage
and here the little bird that struggles
is all courage, pride
echoed in a timeless moment
between flight and flown
newly fluttered from the room of my dreams
and all the while I am watched
by the portrait on the wall.

He who sees through shuttered eyes
says I too should live in moments
of unmeasured time.

New-Born Day

Dawn.

A rattle
of bird feathers.

Shafts of light
cream a step.

A grumbling shift
next door.

Swish-back cat
leaps from sill.

In a cot
eyes blink.

Gourds

In Kent, water from the butt spills
onto her toes in their open sandals
she takes the can, wildly sluicing
baskets trailing pink pelargonium
and temporarily luscious fuscias.

Over in Arizona, at the back of the shacks
in a sandy yard, the succulents
guard their moisture in heavy green sacks
and the gourds are smaller this year
as the heat has calloused their shells.

The Station Clock Or Adoption 1955

The advertisement in the window
read 'Loving home required'.

She studied it for longer than a while
returning to the scrap
of lined and perforated paper
her fingers on a sixpence in her pocket.

Under the perfect halo
of the station clock she met
the ghost of love but cannot keep
whose hooded eyes and shuttered sighs
sob ricochet through the blackest night.

No strings attached
no ribbons, no bows
just a simple wrap
and a photograph exposed.

The child is tucked into a new gilt crib.
Tongue bared, hand furled
but still he hears the tick tock rhythm
of the clock that is no longer there.

Ghost Hunting

Hoisting up the colours
of parapet Earth

tête-à-tête a new sheen
green on half naked soil

shivering off winter's
strip to hound out

the tough old grass
couched for competition

starting like a pistol shot
birds to their nestings go

innocent
of the neighbourhood cats

who sharpen their claws
to practice ghost-hunting.

The Drummer

Summer is falling into autumn.
I defy the A-rhythmic rain, splatting
my consciousness like my child's question
'why raindrops, why not rain drums?'
So we listen to the incessant roll
of the percussionist's tip tap
on every tin top barn,
pattering buckets placed under leaks,
thrumming keyboards of plastic corrugations.

I set the wipers on their fastest speed
watch the leaves as they catch in the blades.
Their hands smear the screen
with an equinoxal message.
I think of centre court tennis
a button pressed, gears cranked
a layer slipped under the sky to the applause
of the Great Rain Drummer
playing an accolade on its skin tight fix.

That night the frost comes with a bitter sleet.
Still, I won't give up on the summer
of my geraniums. Black by morning.
I have allowed them to die.
Their blooms lay slaughtered
no pansied leaf from which to rub a scent
and enjoy my odoured skin hours later.
Not until next summer.

Sea Stars

i

A cormorant on a rock dove deep
his hooked beak caught in an upward flick
neck expanding like an opening gill
swallowing complete
Piscean jaws, fins, scales
leaving no slit in the flawless sea.

ii

I take a tide-full of grains for my hourglass
collect a crystal lens eroded smooth
slip it into the orbit of my eye.
Through it I see the past
where dark clouds speak
of driftwood on the incoming tide.

iii

Again I see a cormorant
when I look down
I see a million starfish
swimming around my feet
like earthly stars.

At night I know the sky for the sea.

Silent Vigil

Standing in a row, a dozen or so
banners held at knee level

to keep us from the bite of wind.
Our placards are rotating

windmills turning
into the faces of passers-by

curious, not a minute to stop
they give a second's stare

to say they know
they've heard it all before

on the living room blare.
So silently

we reveal our message
because silently

time will pass
leaving us breathless

wondering
what we could have done.

Hypothermia

Quarters of icy gulags
for squirrels and mice

a scoring in the airwaves
of a boy's breaking voice

snow pats my back
dribbling a line of shiver

as I tread white sand
heel toe heel toe

I stop for a pulse...watch a dog
pee a yellow crystal cavern

as grainy goose feathers float
I stoop to scoop the ice and laugh

at the trickle tingling my throat
like melting glaciers

lozenges petrifying
in molecular quick-link.

Sky fleece from snow
I lie down on fresh white linen

for a perfect sleep.

Heart Of The Beach

The beach lay printless,
tide idle in retreat
buffing at fragments of stone,
jewels for a setting sand.

Warm for the earliness of day,
a breeze of gulls at their business
rivet the cliffs

a flotsam bottle, a float,
a piece of blue rope,
coarse shingle with a glint,
sea glass greens and

a gleaming corpuscle … pumping red
anemone, jelly fish, a man o' war?,

I look out on a sea of questions…
Could it be a human heart
left behind to haunt the beach?

But then, who wouldn't lose their heart
to such a paradise?

Gypsy

Leaning into the arms
of the elm, I nestle up high
and steal a look.

Green waves hide me
reveal me
to the Gypsies magic circle

where dogs loll
and gnaw
at their bitten paws.

Polished chrome
sends out rays
of reflected sun.

A kettle steams
to the clink
of sharpening knives.

Over in the ragwort fields
ponies
nudge at chaff

tan-faced boys roll
in the snaky grass
and scrap

between broken cars.
I catch a shout
in the net of my tree

my foot slips,
the earth slaps
under my scraped knee

Mud!
And I'm home.
'Just like a gypsy' says Gran

'Like the one who called
with a posy
and a promise

that a boy
will be born'.
Mother awakes

rubs her belly,
eyes the silver coin
in her palm.

Twirling The Shovel

I should have been weeding the garden that day
but when I went to the shed I began to dance
waltzing the rake
one two three
one two three
spinning a jig with a hoe
toe heel toe
twirling the spade to a tune in my head

then the wind caught hold of the door
and a pulse of light tapped my shoulder.

As I zipped in a blind street dance
between the crab-apple and pear
 'Nice day for it',
my neighbour said with a wink
but I didn't care
as I jived with a fern in my mouth

Circadian Echoes

The shortest day, the longest night
a glitch in the Circadian rhythm
a deep sleep by an open fire
the smouldered scents of apple
a curl of smoke from a beeswax candle.

As ancient as the Sun's first ebb
when the man with a collier's face
crossed a threshold with a single piece
and as he leapt, first right, then left,
the jig of life began.

So let us dance the feast,
sing in the bringing of the Season
while the Earth stretches
tilting her axial arc so far
from the giant Sol star.

Such brief hours make dreamtime
as the cold light makes sepia
of the shadows that fade in the Arctic glow
but in our sleepy hearts we recognise
the magic of the Solstice spell.

First Love, Island Cafe

Alice wipes a table
seized by the urn's reflection
she rubs a smudge
checks her hair
lips fatten in the cylinder's face
flicks a cornered crumb
eyes widen under convex lids.

Across the road Joe kneels
under an arch
face masked, shielded
from the cobalt flames
he rises to his own reflection
blushes a grin
sheds his gauntlets

he strides across the camber

a wink in a seal's eye

his steps rivet

a door swings a beam

her collar bone catches the light.

How The World Was Made

When I hear the clink of sail-tops
shifting in their roost
disquieting the part of me
that longs to buffer out
to wing across the wildest seas
and find an anchorage
from which to scrutinize
all three hundred and sixty degrees.

Then I'll dive into the deep
renew my cells, baptise them
one by one until
my body's salts will crystallize
in notes and words that sing
a song of fledgling birds
whose flights delight in joys
of life within a soft bone cage.

And as my ribs float singly loose
I'll run the wind
through beams of operatic roofs
where dreams come true
in nimbus wisps revealing facts
like how the world was made
with love, and then,
my uncaged heart will weep.

Sixteen

Inside the church we dread in vaults
the twist of the dead shot iron latch.

She arrives on a rickshaw of white lilies
that dare to flout their fecundity.

This is no stretch limo on its way to the prom
no dream boat waits to take her arm

she travels alone in her final mode
a full length version in beech, soon to be ash.

We stand back, held in by our best black chokers,
the ones we left hanging in tied tongues

at the backs of our wardrobes.
The priest tells how sixteen years ago

she cried as he sprinkled her pulsing fontanel.
We laugh, inept, not meaning to be callow

with her so quiet, guarded by four stout candles.

Cut And Paste Face

I can't place your face
as if it's been cut/
pasted onto my page.
Questions scroll before my eyes
in a list of FAQs.

Did we once swop secrets on a train?
I remember the moving landscape.

Speak of 'two for the price' at the till?
Your lips miming.

The nurse at the clinic?
An inch of face over a speculum.

A bus stop?
We complained but still we waited.

Or are you simply the likeness
of someone I once knew?

When I walk on, your face follows.
It comes away peeled and whole.

The Blessing

After you were born, we planted a tree
– a sapling pear.

The glint of a spade in the afternoon sun
a signal for the soil to nourish with tenderness

a ritual renewed by a new-born's snuffle.
In time the blossom is as white as your flesh

is pink. Fragile heads that flicker in the breeze
in a salutation to Hera.

Then come the fruits, kernels of creation.
Each one a single drop of tear.

Time waits for the flight of an angel's wing
as our abundant crop hails his first cry

our blessing – and so you were born,
a slow motion memory of pear parting tree.

Over And Over

Over and Over
the ripple tide waves
form crescents
like the islands of an Irish bay
conjured from the moulds
of tundral frost.

Over and Over
designed in a time
when the land shrank back
with a slide and retreat
of the Great Glacial Ice.
At the lowest tide
sand bumps bruise my arches
as I trace a path of patterns.

Over and Over
I walk mistakes into the sand
as if all of life is a mosaic
of broken Romanesque tiles
that I am trying to fit
into a long forgotten place
of dragons teeth and Celtic knots
when all around are hints
clues that I ignore in the blueprints
of the shells on every sea snail.
Over and Over.

Where The Cinnabar Moth...

I

Gliding the West Riding
where the wild Pennines rise
amongst foothills, barren mounds
of moorland forked in clefts
green shoots emerge
the bark of the silver birch shimmers.
Streams run clear until sudden storms
wash acid from the earth
and a single shaft of sunlight pierces
the brown tinted waters.
Villages are dug into this once glacial land
their rows of stone houses
plume and feather out along the valley bottoms
dormitories for the old Victorian Mills.

Silence falls as we drift
towards a single familiar valley
where intrepid hikers meander
through steep heather edged in brackish bogs
where in the summertime rowan trees burst their ripe
berries, kingfishers loop the loop.

Coming in to land we see a church
a Tyrolean tower crowns the trees
above a patch of land uncommonly smooth
where doll people drag their trolleys
small white balls catch the light
landing on a smooth woven cloth of green.

A Mill, alone on the edge of the moor
is the ghost of brightly lit 'works'
where treaded floors are steeped
in a century of oil and grease
where boilers chugged through the night
a stained chimney smoked a black belch
a siren sounded for the five o'clockers shifters
their wooden clogs hollow on the tarmac.
Ghosts. Gone now with the final shift.
Offices empty, machinery dismantled
a site of rapid dilapidation
along a path of scattered remnants
bobbins with thread attached
the swatches of samples
for the shadowy salesmen to flout.

II

The stream trickles, gushes its chosen course
shoulders a torrent, disgorges branches
runs underground through a set of weirs
that once controlled the flow
gates clogged with twigs, feathers
the odd beer can.

Persistent Nature reclaims.

Concrete cracks as new shoots push
form crazy pavements.
In the summer the flowers, grasses,
weeds throw out their seeds
as birds nest, a badger makes a set

a fox crosses the path
always at a sideways lope
neck stooped, head below the echoes.

The stream is purged of toxic dye.
Trout hide in the gloom of overhanging foliage at the
approach of a pterodactyl shadow.

Stork legs are stilled as a fish in free-fall
relaxes, hypnotized by the caress of the current attracting
the attention of a beady eyed heron.

III

Pluvial mists seep and snake
into rivulets that conspire
and steep beyond dew point.

Sheep fleeced of their coats
graze and scour
the sponge acidic earth
where apprentices to beavers
weave sticks and shuttle stones
with an ancient instinct.

In the stream a swatch of wool
bleeds a streak of scarlet dye
as it puddles, it spins cumulus pink.

Skeins and scraps of shapeless vats
litter the hard set concrete
corrugations of asbestos

protrude green shoots
from a patchwork of pits
trapped beneath the brambles.

Sudden death slopes in a gully
of discarded cans and quick-love
condoms where the innocent
sorrel and primrose breed
quince and crabapple
flaunt their luminous wares.

A damselfly hovers a stream
blooming with chemicals
aniline and rosaniline mixed
with iodides turns sapphire
to indigo, as yet unmatched
by the blue jay's plume.

IV

Windows bricked in
blocked out blinded and mute
ledges of mossy beds for sleepy birds
old echoes heard by owls
whiskered by a curious fox
rabbit soft noses test the wind

Tiny creatures work the bales
where the striped caterpillar
of the cinnabar moth
gorges on ragwort veined in toxin

then licks its gumless lips
for essences of arsenic.

A gothic statue impales the land
With a hundred feet of circular brick
a chimney exalted by a blackened brim.

The hopper telescopes the sky
edged rust teeters on an easel
its vortex scratch-sucks
the wind to an audience of clouds
who spit percussive droplets
playing triangle and kettle drum.

A badger, curious in the moonlight
sniffs the old brass plate
buffed by a passing breeze
a door ushers, lifts a ripple of paper
on the old mahogany desk
poached from a bygone Empire

polished with shellac of dust
grooved with the ghosts
of in and out trays
a piece of coral
and a sea horse trapped
eternally in a weight of glass

restrains the history notes
of paper thin orders
picked, despatched for cash.

V

Along the road to the mill
is a flap flap notice
on a lamppost
where a faceless dog
cocks a leg
to the diggers
the 'dozers
the demolition crew

artists of graffiti
spray their territory
lunchtime lovers
tryst in the shade
synchronizing
rendezvous
Fords escort
wide-eyed girls
blow fat exhausts
smoke hash
to the crack
of their skateboard wheels

as all the while
a float of gnats
hover in the bat-eyed dusk
and the birds on the ledge
fold down for the night.

By Crepuscular...

I mean not merely the creatures
of the faded light but every nuance
that threads the twilight edges
fraying at the start of night
whose tassel-ends give flight
to the closing day

when evening wears
a cloak of royal blue
majestically empowered
with streak-red threads
diminished by the arrival
of a child in sky blue pink

pyjamas who is staying up
to watch the punk cicadas
in the damp grass
tune their orchestrations
with harp-legged twangs
that reverberate until

a heavy in black complains
and all crepuscular creatures
slink off home until dawn
with little more than a brief adieu
and a shake of the pin-pricked
hand of the stars,
that's what I mean...

Dead Wood Scrolls

Ghost sailors blow their horns
through full-rigged trees
as Freya's falcon lands
in the forest of the silver birch.

I hear the distant rumble
of the chariots of death
the silhouetted riders
the two black cats of myth.

I scent the sanguine sap
as I slip heel down a scree
to a clearing in the wood
lumber high with the slain.

The valkyrie's sons approach in a 4x4
come to assess their haul
of half trunked cores
to count their golden rings.

At their feet lay dappled peelings
the hieroglyphic scrolls
a cache of secret scrawls
beneath a cloak of charcoal mist.

Small Fry

Bubbles rap a rhythmic river.
Rocks syncopate the surface
with friction-less liquidity
where even the fisherman's judder line
runs thumb-smooth.

Water, stone, scissors
cut free with slip-glisten fluidity
through dash-head torrents
where landscapers greet with hollow pats
wet rock on wet rock
guards of the borders
sentinels to a force
that passes for a running army.
It could be anything,
finned, gilled, boned,
of fleshly components.

In the sludge of under-stones
the tiny creatures of under-world
in part crepuscular
seek the dark, the deep dark
where tomb stones block
the filter light of the river green soup.

Wing, scale, invertebrate
slip-minnows stickle
in the pooling shadows
boatmen brake, skaters dance
on a skin-thin surface with fine-hair legs

water-fleas beetle
in their name-sake element
trout brood brown depths
rudder the mainstream
where planktonic microbes
begin the chain of sustenance
for the Overlords of River.

White water, rapid light
a branch lips a bend
lifting a crescent of spume
a froth lathers loose bark
criss-crossing
a weir made by the wetland architects
— a successful re-introduction.
Here the water is acid brown.
Peat deep. A hint of a trap
where the whirligigs circle
and circle and mesmerise.

But on a mild day,
like today, it is a spawning pool
a safe nursery for the small fry in its well.

Mr Noisy

In the Quiet Zone
the tinny rhythms
swarm like flies
around plugged ears
a page, exaggerates a turn
jolts a head that rears
snorts at a half glimpsed cutting.

We attune to the flat flack
of the metal breaking chink
of Osman's trolley
forced into retreat
by the arrival
of a large-lettered station.

New passengers invade
the old resolve
to keep their contracts
of no eye-contact
don't dare sit here
while my bag squats
the next seat free
under the LCD script
scrolling 'not reserved'.

Relieved, we settle back
and hope they've read
the other sign
the one about the Quiet Zone.

Tight lipped
we gaze at soothing hills
assured the flash of red
prohibits use of mobile phones.

Passing in and out
of trackside lives
we are interrupted
by a junglists tune
erupting from a headrest
announcing to us all
that **he** is on the train.

The Waiting Room

My lady waits at the table head.
Bride-in waiting.

The mice are hungry, the cake disgorged
the hind legs of a cockroach rattle
as a meal of a fly comes loose from a beam.

My quick eye calculates in hanks
cordage for warp, threads for weft.
I bridle up, ready to sling my net
from the limb of the stilled hour hand.

I lick my lips around the word 'embellishment'.

With the effort of birthing I let out my silks
tautly tatting, inventing the wheel
with spirals that drip by the light of the moon
fine-edged in parallel hoops.

I cast off. We wait.

A Pot Of Tea

We are watching through plate glass
as we inspect the dregs of Earl Grey

in the bottom of our cups we talk
the socks off dachshunds in a park

we lift our faces to finalise
the plans to resolve the situation

in Afghanistan and furthermore
we register the rise and fall

of monetary markets
and when it comes to equal pay

and equal rights, believe us
with scimitar lips we cut

huge swathes into the butter curls
for these, our toasted teacake moments.

The Fine Line

Here on the sill is a dish
that holds a bar of Sunlight.
The copper on the stove
steams a hum
a washboard waits
its weekly tune.

It's Monday
and the kitchen has become
an exotic sauna
for a galley slave in a housecoat
to heave-ho the sheets
with her wooden boiler stick.

Plunging, lifting, draining
swilling a blue-bag rinse
she wrings the drops
and feeds what's left
through the rubber lips
of the flat mangle squash.

The fabric of her upper arm
stretches taut
as she quick-flicks out
into the westerly breeze
threading wet cloths
on a prayer flag line.

But when it rains
she saddles the horse
that patiently waits
in front of the hand-stoked fire.
Only then does our sweated slave
rest the bones of her back.

Rocking in her chair
on the new scrubbed deck
she reaches for the dresser
takes the brown glass bottle
and with a quick-flip
pours out a yard of ale.

Her upper lip is a fine line of froth.

Dust

I open the flower press
release the dust remains.
Anemones. Their stalks
once refracted in a glass bowl,
petals of red, indigo,
creamy white, centres black.

Behind the curtain Nana lay dying
and I thought she'd slipped
into morphinous sleep, so I too
slipped out. Later, on the table
were the fallen petals
and a vase full of tears.

Rising Scents

On the allotment the peas are ready
my first job aged 4
a thumb-push opens a pod
I gaze at the tiny bedfellows
held in by their lap straps.

It doesn't seem right
but a green pea in the mouth
is the taste of the colour of summer.

Now, I pass you discs of cucumber
stripes of pepper
you press them with milk gums
the flavours explode
your mouth is smudged with a smile.

Bread dough squeezes
knuckling through our fingers
sticky, we add more flour
wrestling 'til yeast scents rise.

The Trunk

She gave me a string
of rosebuds, cream,
scented with almonds

inherited from an uncle
who'd stalked
the plains of Africa.

Too heavy
for my sapling neck
they adorned my doll

Angelina, and when
the threading
cord had broken

I placed them in a trunk
where they lay
for years until the day

when a man on the TV
pointed to a carcass
captured, de-tusked

discarded by poachers.
Tipping over the trunk
I let the ivory beads run free.

Crow's feet

I swim across a lake where folds of mist
flop the water's surface in clockwork waves.
The wind buffs my goose face flesh but
underneath, neck down, I am a constant cool.

A sun break lifts a swell, cracks a smile
of my crow's feet as I lark into the current.
Fine petals braise in the breeze, russet edged
their stems coursed with green blood.

On the bank, a blink of daisies
turn to mime the yellow of day.
By winter, their corms will be underground
dormant to the ricochet of the jackdaw's

hammer that skewers the severed stalks.
Tough nature, but as if in spite, a shaft of light
reaches through cloud, gently polishing
each leaf of holly with the varnish of the sun.

On Harris

Rain, Hebrides

under the Atlantic ruff
dog rose on the rocks
blowing beyond the watermark
soft peat, beach of shells
tiny as stitchwort
crisp underfoot, duneland
threaded with marram
pastureland daisies, campion
eyebright
where the waders breed
a lapwing, a crackling corncrake
a pewit on the machair.

As butting sheep rip the land
a black char scours the bones
a redshank shims its call
and the sky answers
in blue vapour that falls
upon a stained glass sea, cut

by a single boat.

Constance

I do believe
that the sky
is always
blue
up there
beyond the clouds
as clear
as your love
is to me

but how can I
be sure
that when the earth
has turned
on its nightly axis
that dawn
will always
break
into that same sapphire sky.

Stone, Water, Air, Fire, Peace

I see a pebble at the bottom of a stream.
The water is unaware of a rock
in its buffeting brook, the stone
is an island, a meditation,
untroubled by each gurgle
and the water's feathered touch
merely varnishes the stone's resilience.
Here is peace in the heart of a stone.

The lake is deep and clear, stilled
until a bird dips briefly in
to power its upward flight.
A wing drips droplets across a mirror
sending spiralled waves, that wheel
and wheel in fading ripple ends.
Circles overlap until replete
the sheen returns. One tranquil surface.

In the trees the wind catches leaves
waving their green in semaphore
to no-one in particular
caressing each leaf until it dives
to snatch mist from the mouths of strangers
taking the clouds of living breath
to a place where waves are lulled
under a plateau of softly spoken air.

When the night is still I hear a crackle
magic wands in their first heat.
A show of palm hands to the flames
consuming within stone bounds.
Burn, cleanse, flame by flame,
fire into wood into charcoal
returned to carbon Earth.
By morning there is a strange black peace.

Curtains

The sun beams
through floral curtains
where a bee is trapped
between net and drape
silhouetting a circle
of printed blossoms.

Should I tell him
about the trick,
that the flowers are not real?
No. It is the drone end
of summer and soon the bee

will leave on a bubble
that expires in the breeze.
Over on the fabric pond
I see a pair
of stitched damselflies
wings bonded

electrified bodies
zip from reed to reed.
Quickly they fade
into dustings of dew
where even the winkle-end
of sun cannot reach.

Ageless Angel

Diaphanous tranquillity
    pervades the serenity
        of your face
            as I watch
                a creaseless brow
                    forehead
              no enmity
           the ageless face
        of child asleep.

    Nose rumpled
        flickered lids
            belie a dream
                your mind
                    betranced
                dissolved
           to spaces
      far away.
              Fret not, sweet love
                be still.

Lover's Touch

Skin of old age
the thin translucent
paper kind.
Your absent mindful
strokes know well
the tender turns,
the folds refolding
in subcutaneous pleasure.
Lover of the latter years
you watch my mind
channel, re-channel,
waver on a brink.

Ocean

The sucking ocean
pulls at my fluidity.
All the elements
of birth and death
meet here
at the shoreline.

Indigo Dreams Publishing
132, Hinckley Road
Stoney Stanton
Leicestershire
LE9 4LN
www.indigodreams.co.uk

Papers used by Indigo Dreams are recyclable products made from wood grown in sustainable forests following the guidance of the Forest Stewardship Council.